The Ultimate
Panda
Book for Kids

100+ Panda Facts, Photos, Quiz + More

Jenny Kellett

BELLANOVA

MELBOURNE · SOFIA · BERLIN

Copyright © 2023 by Jenny Kellett
The Ultimate Panda Book for Kids
ISBN: 978-619-264-009-5
Bellanova Books
www.bellanovabooks.com

All rights reserved. No part of this book may be reproduced in any form by any electronic or mechanical means including photocopying, recording, or information storage and retrieval without permission in writing from the author.

Contents

Panda Facts 6
Panda Quiz 66
Quiz Answers 71
Word Search Puzzle 72
Sources 75

Introduction

They're big, fluffy and ridiculously cute, which are just some of the reasons why pandas are our favourite animals. Pandas are one of the world's most at-risk animals, which means it's more important than ever to understand more about them, their habitats and the things that put them at risk.

Learn more about the Giant Panda and its unrelated friend the Red Panda in this fun book of panda facts. Then, test your knowledge at the end in our panda quiz!

Let's get started...

A Giant Panda enjoying some bamboo.
Credit: Jay Wennington

Panda Facts

When we talk about pandas, we are generally referring to the Giant Panda. However, there are also Red Pandas, that we will talk about soon!

•••

An adult panda can weigh over 45kg (100 lb) and be 1.5 metres (5 ft) long.

•••

Pandas are great at climbing trees. They can start climbing when they are just seven months old.

New born panda cubs at the panda breeding station in Chengdu, China.

Credit: Pascal Müller

Pandas are great, confident swimmers. They love splashing around to cool down.

• • •

Pandas have six fingers! This extra thumb helps them to mould bamboo into an easier-to-eat shape.

• • •

When pandas are born they look quite different! They have pink skin, no fur and are completely blind. Their famous black and white colours come around three weeks later.

A hungry panda in the wild.

A Qinling "Brown" Panda, the only one in captivity in the world. Credit: AilieHM

Not all pandas are black and white! There are also brown and white pandas, although these are quite rare.

• • •

Pandas are lazy creatures. They really do just eat and sleep most of the day.

If you want to see a panda in the wild or at a zoo, you need to get up early as this is when they are most active.

...

The laziness of pandas is one reason why they are so rare: they don't prioritise mating. Also, there are only one to three days per year that a female can naturally become pregnant!

...

Pandas can only be found in the wild in China. Most pandas are found in southwestern China, although their habitat is shrinking.

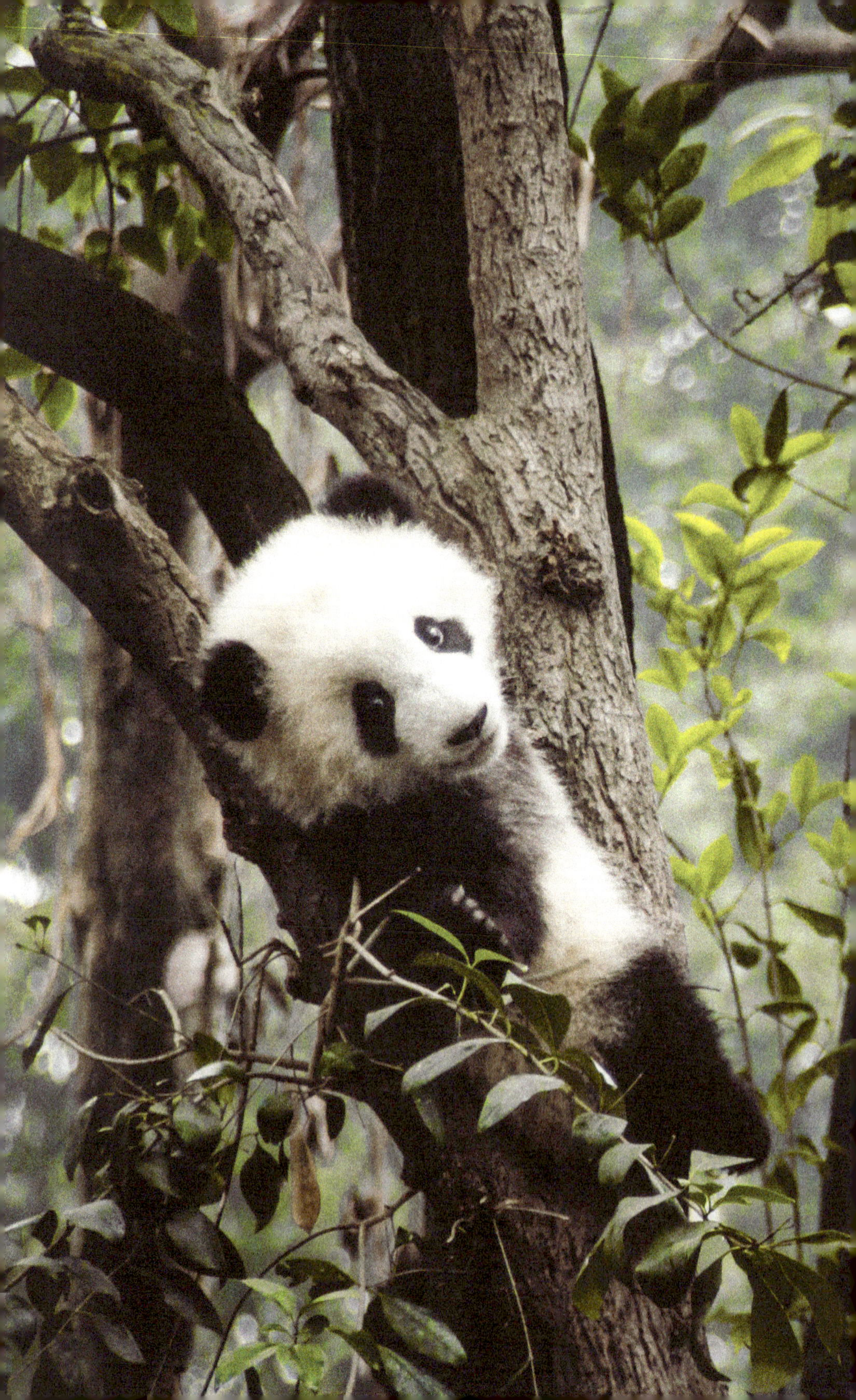

A giant panda cub chilling in a tree at the Chengdu Research Base of Giant Panda Breeding. *Credit: Theodor Lundqvist*

There's a reason why so many photos of pandas include some bamboo. Pandas spend up to 14 hours a day eating their favourite food! During this time, pandas eat 12-38 kg of bamboo.

...

Bamboo doesn't contain many calories or nutrients, which is why pandas have to eat so much of it.

...

Pandas are technically omnivores (meaning they eat meat and plants). However, 99% of their diet is made up of bamboo. They only occasionally eat small fish and animals.

While pandas have the teeth and digestive systems to be carnivores, modern pandas no longer have the energy to hunt down prey.

• • •

In the past, pandas had predators like the sabre-toothed tiger, so they needed to be able to defend themselves.

• • •

The panda's scientific name is *Ailuropoda melanoleuca*. If you translate it, this means black and white cat-foot!

Scientists still don't know how long pandas live in the wild, but in captivity, they live to around 30 years old.

• • •

The oldest living panda in captivity was 38 years old.

• • •

When they are born, baby pandas are only 15cm (6 in) long.

• • •

Pandas are largely solitary creatures and are quite happy spending most of their lives alone.

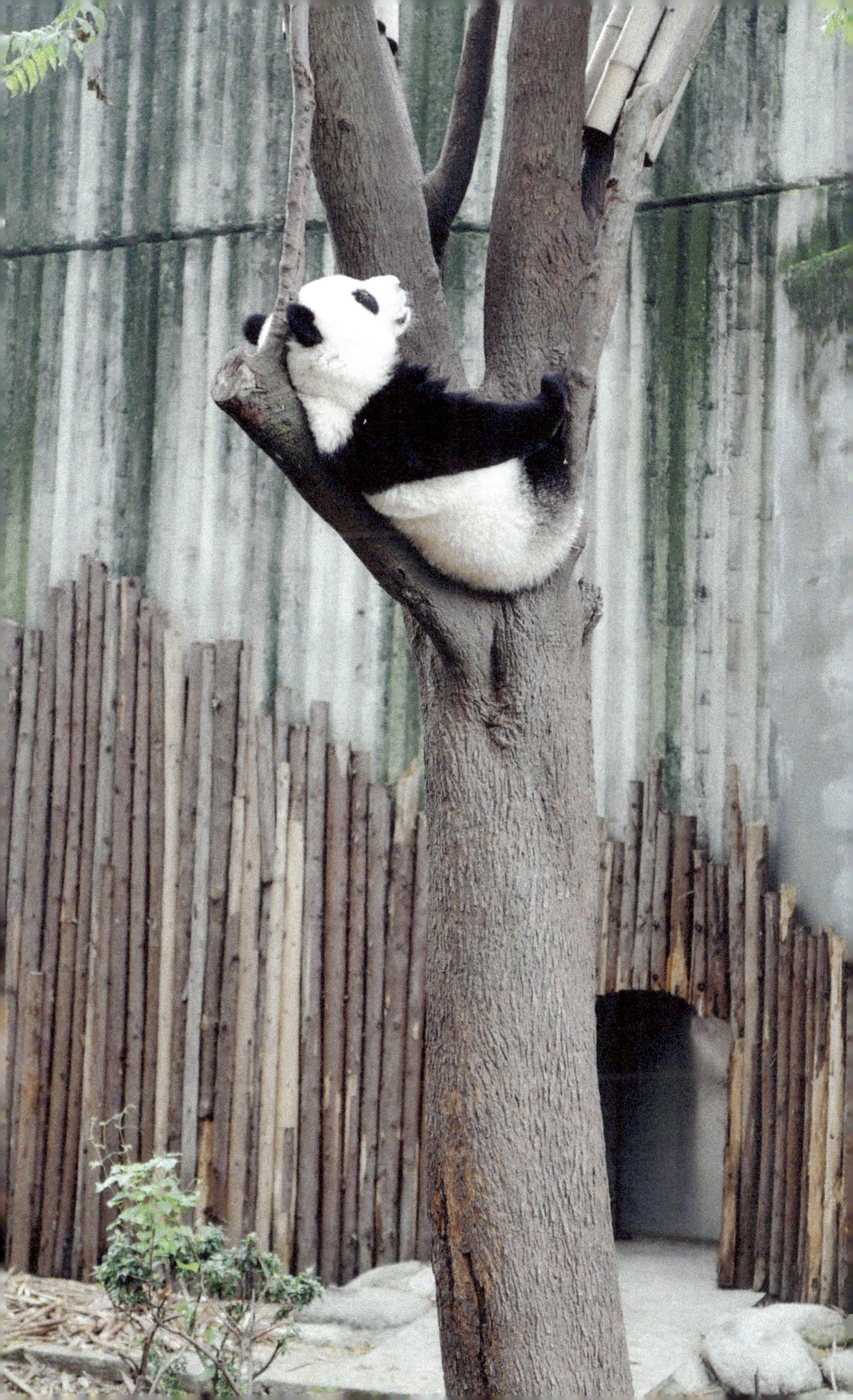

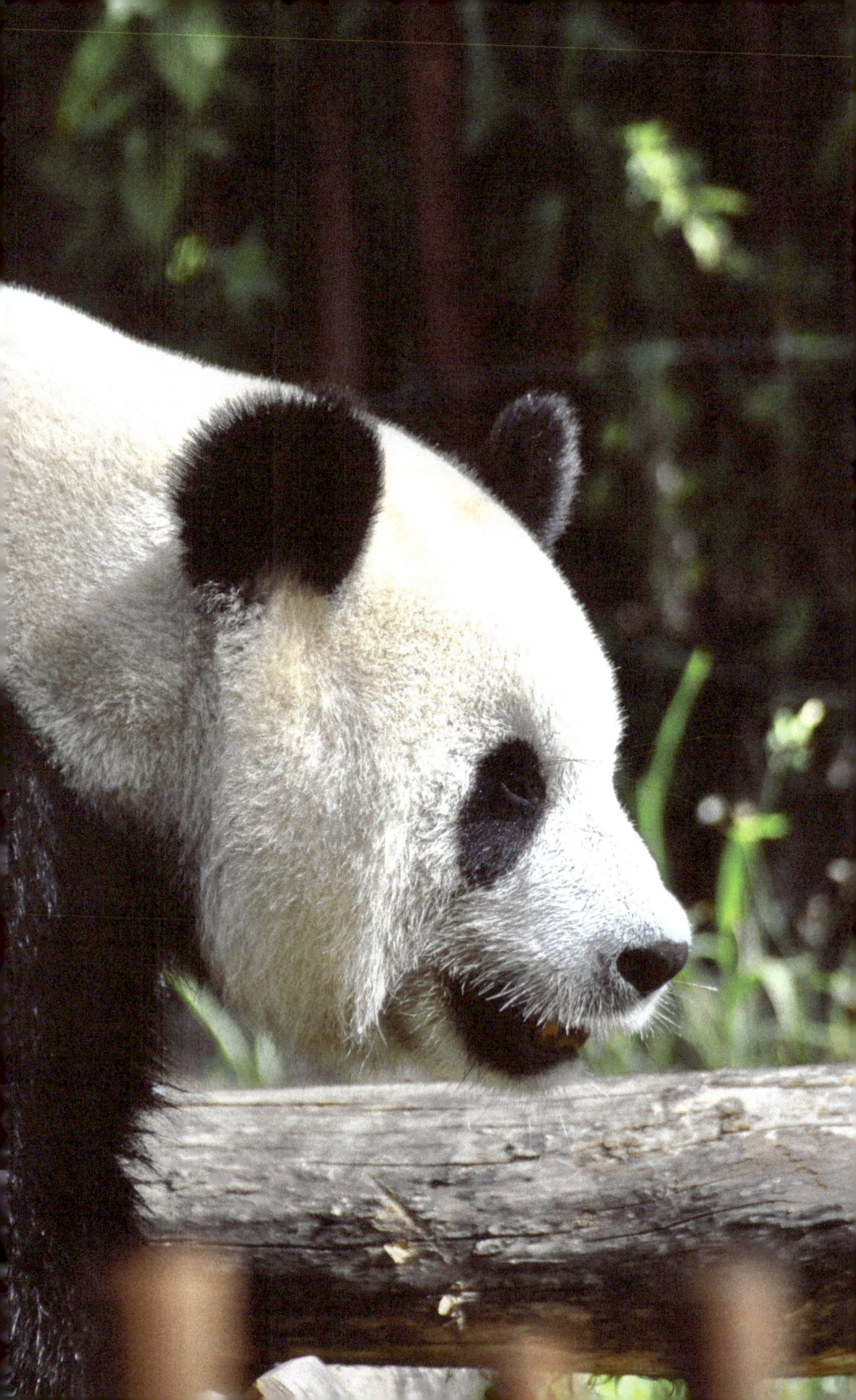

Female pandas give birth to one or two cubs every two years. Two cubs are most common, but in the wild, only the stronger cub survives.

• • •

Researchers in Chengdu have successfully experimented with swapping out panda cubs so the mothers can raise two cubs. This project is helping to increase the number of pandas in the wild.

• • •

Cubs stay with their mothers for 18 months before they set off on their own.

An adult Giant Panda. *Credit: Chen Wu*

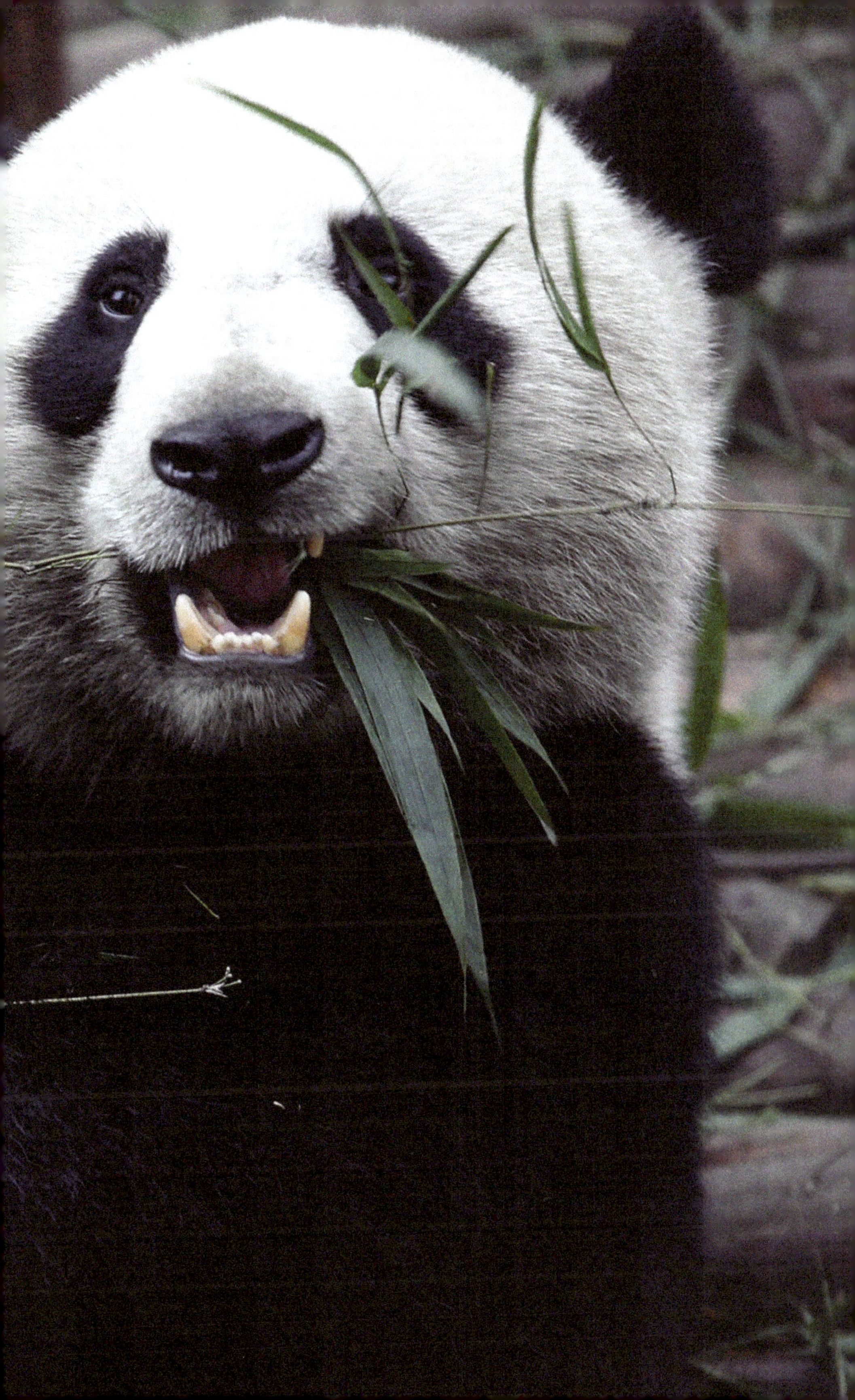

Unlike other types of bears, pandas don't hibernate. Instead, they move down the mountains to find warmer temperatures.

• • •

Pandas can't store fat, which is one of the reasons why they can't hibernate.

• • •

With all the bamboo that pandas eat, comes a lot of poop! A panda can poop as much as 28kg per day.

A sleeping panda at Berlin Zoo.

Credit: Chris Curry

As well as a large quantity of poop, they are super regular too! They usually poop around 40 times a day.

•••

In the past, unchewed bamboo found in panda poop was collected and turned into souvenirs such as picture frames.

•••

Even if a panda is born in captivity overseas, it remains the property of the Chinese Government and must be returned.

A panda eating bamboo at Memphis Zoo.

Credit: Joshua J. Cotten

Zoos must pay around $1 million to 'borrow' a panda from China for ten years.

• • •

Pandas are a threatened species. Sadly, there are only around 1,000 of them left in the wild. However, some scientists, believe that wild panda populations are increasing.

• • •

Pandas had been on the endangered species list since 1990 but were moved to the 'vulnerable' list in 2016, largely thanks to successful breeding programs in China and overseas.

A happy panda with his stash of bamboo.

Credit: Qinghong Shen

THE ULTIMATE PANDA BOOK FOR KIDS

Pandas at the Chengdu Panda Base in Chengdu, China. Credit: Sonorama

Sadly, as China's population rapidly grows, more and more of the panda's habitat is removed and it is harder for them to survive in the wild.

• • •

Most panda cubs are born in August.

• • •

Archaeologists have found evidence from fossils that pandas lived 1 to 2 million years ago. In the past, pandas could be found across almost all of China. Now, there are just small communities in remote areas around the Tibetan foothills.

Pandas walk with their toes in-turned. This characteristic is called 'pigeon-toed'.

...

While most humans will cringe at the thought of licking metal, pandas love it! Zookeepers have found that pandas love licking copper and iron bowls.

David Taylor, an expert on pandas, wrote that *"An ancient reputation as a licker and eater of copper and iron came from a liking for dishes or cooking pots in dwellings of Chinese peasants."*.

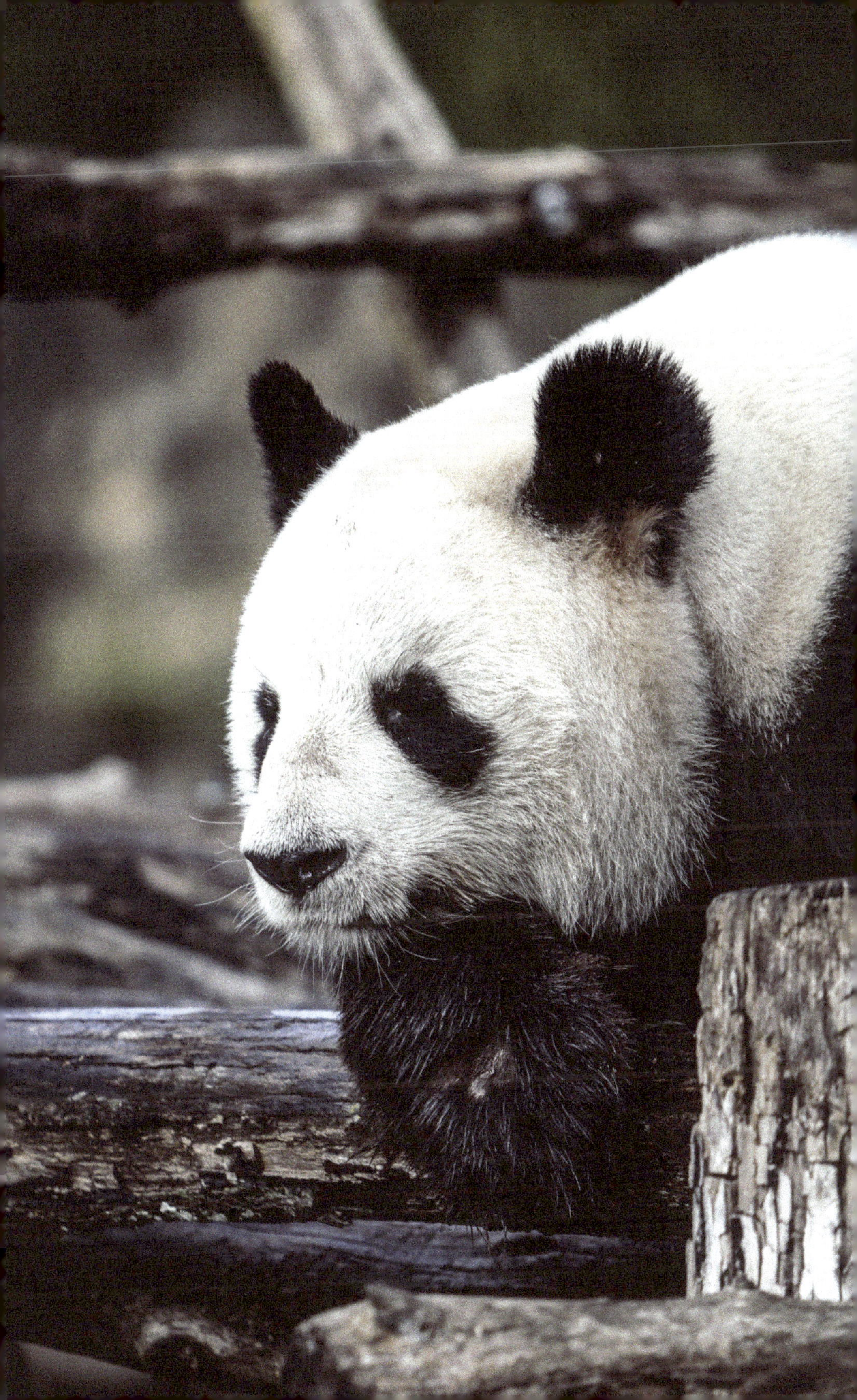

The famous panda logo of the WWF (Worldwide Fund for Nature), was designed after Chi Chi, a giant panda that lived at London Zoo from 1958-1972.

• • •

The first panda ever born into captivity was at Beijing zoo in 1963.

• • •

Pandas that are kept in captivity often enjoy eating fruits, such as apples. In the summer zookeepers in China feed the pandas frozen apples to help cool them down.

A hungry panda. Credit: Isolate Create

Just as cats like to mark their territory by peeing on objects, pandas do the same. Male pandas, though, do a handstand against a tree while marking their territories, to get it as high as possible!

...

When panda cubs are born the circles around their eyes are round. As they get older, these circles become more like a teardrop shape.

...

The red panda and the giant panda may have similar names, but the red panda actually belongs to the raccoon family, while the panda is in the bear family.

Pandas having a snack together.
Credit: Chi King

Despite the red panda and giant panda being entirely different species, they do have several similarities. They are both native to Asia and can be found in some of the same habitats.

...

Pandas and red pandas also both have an extended wrist bone, which acts like a thumb.

...

Red pandas, however, spend most of their time living in trees. They only usually come down to mate.

Although pandas can stand upright, they can't support themselves for very long. Panda bones are very dense and weigh twice as much as most other animals their size.

• • •

Pandas have great spatial memory. This means that they are good at remembering locations. This is important for finding their way back to their favourite patch of bamboo.

• • •

A female cub becomes an adult when she is five years old. Male cubs take up to seven years to reach adulthood.

A Red Panda relaxing in a tree.

When a panda becomes pregnant, she starts building a nest out of bamboo in preparation for the birth.

• • •

There are around 300 captive pandas around the world. Every panda is part of a breeding program to help prevent them from extinction.

• • •

Pandas have plantigrade feet. This means that they walk on all parts of their feet — like humans. Cats and dogs walk with their weight on their toes.

Researchers have found that pandas use 11 different calls. Four of them are used only when searching for a mate.

• • •

A panda mother is 800 times the size of its newborn cub!

• • •

The fur of a baby panda is very soft and fluffy. It gets more coarse as it gets older.

• • •

Male pandas are about 10% larger than females.

A curious panda cub. Credt: Sharon Ang

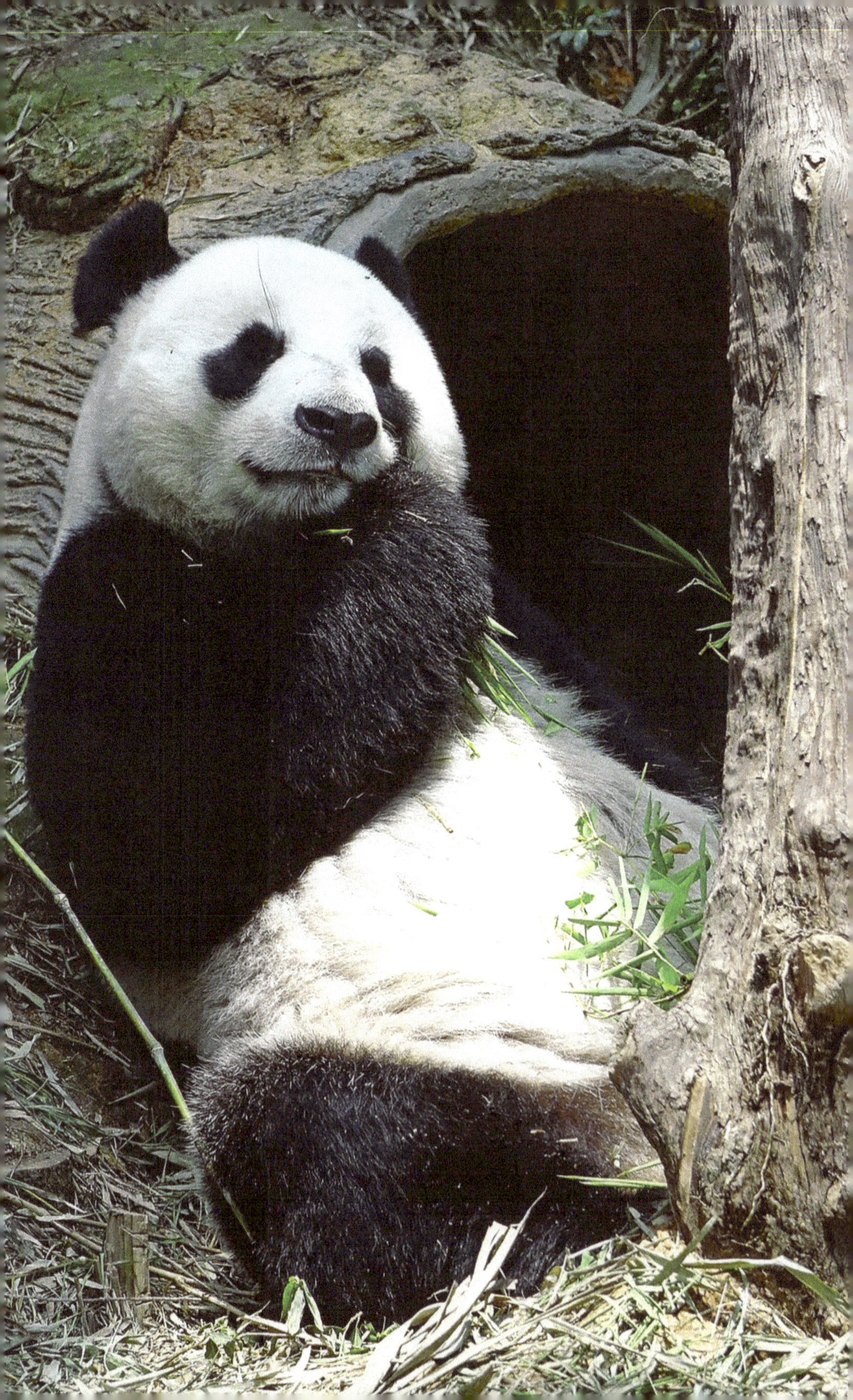

If you try to eat bamboo, it will most likely be very painful! Fortunately, pandas have a special lining on their throats to protect them from splinters.

• • •

Pandas have 42 teeth and go through two sets in their lifetime — like humans.

• • •

Why is a panda called a panda? Nobody knows for sure, but many believe it comes from the Nepalese word ponya, which refers to its extra thumb, or adapted wrist bone.

President Richard Nixon was the first U.S. president to visit China. As a gift, the Chinese leader sent him two pandas, which were then placed in Washington DC's National Zoo.

• • •

After mating, females chase the male out of her territory.

• • •

There are over 300 types of bamboo in China, and pandas have their favourites. Umbrella, arrow and golden bamboo are their top choices. Pandas need to eat at least two varieties of bamboo to stay healthy.

A sleeping panda at San Diego Zoo.

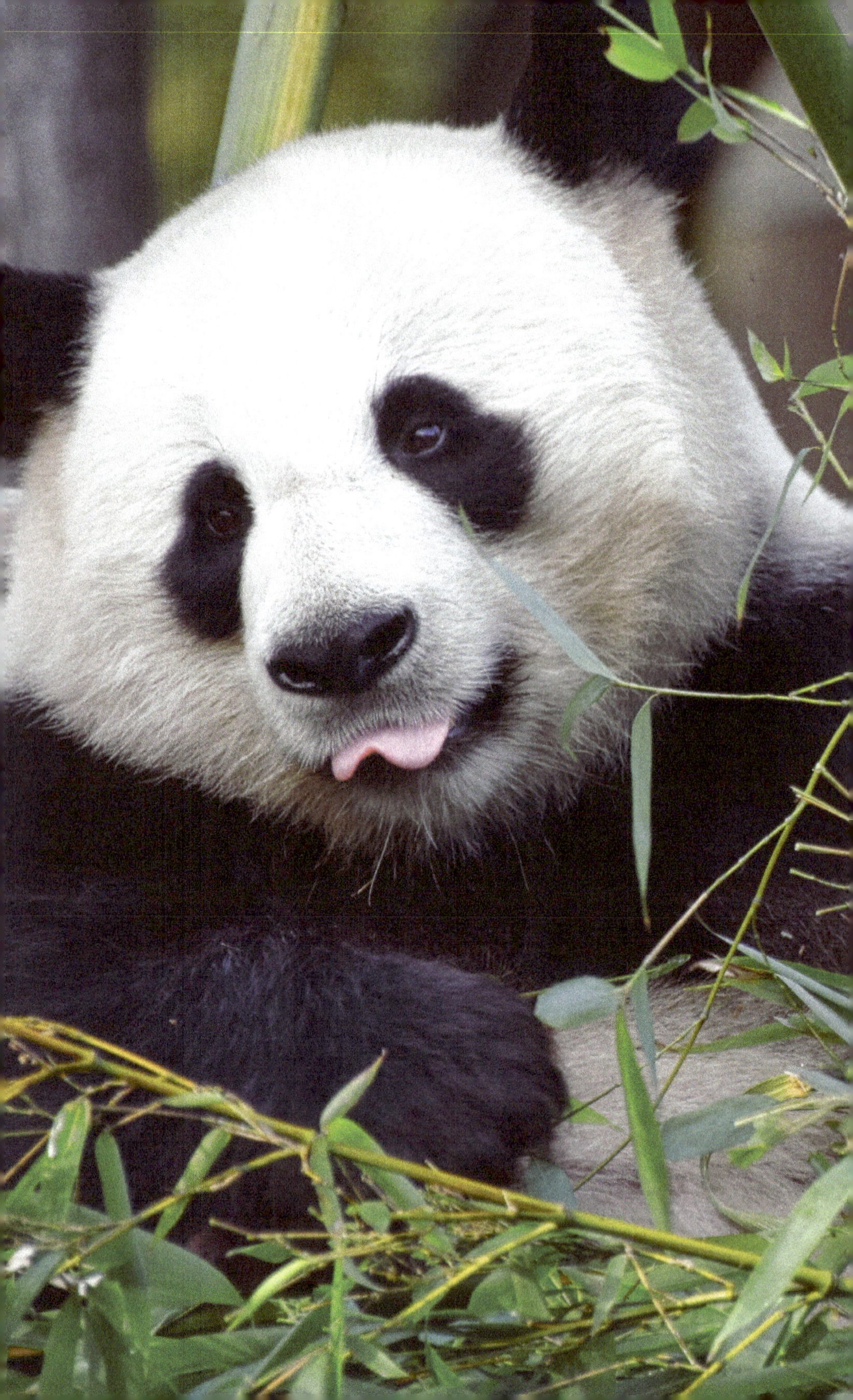

A panda's face may look chubby, but it is actually incredibly muscly. They need these muscles to help them chew through the tough bamboo.

• • •

It takes just 40 seconds for a panda to peel and eat a bamboo shoot.

• • •

It costs around five times as much to take care of a panda than an elephant in a zoo.

Pandas don't have many natural enemies, due to their large size. However, their cubs can often be at risk from snow leopards and other opportunistic hunters.

• • •

Under its fur, the panda has black skin where its fur is black and pink skin where its fur is white.

• • •

Panda cubs drink their mother's milk for the first year of their lives but are able to chew small pieces of bamboo after six months.

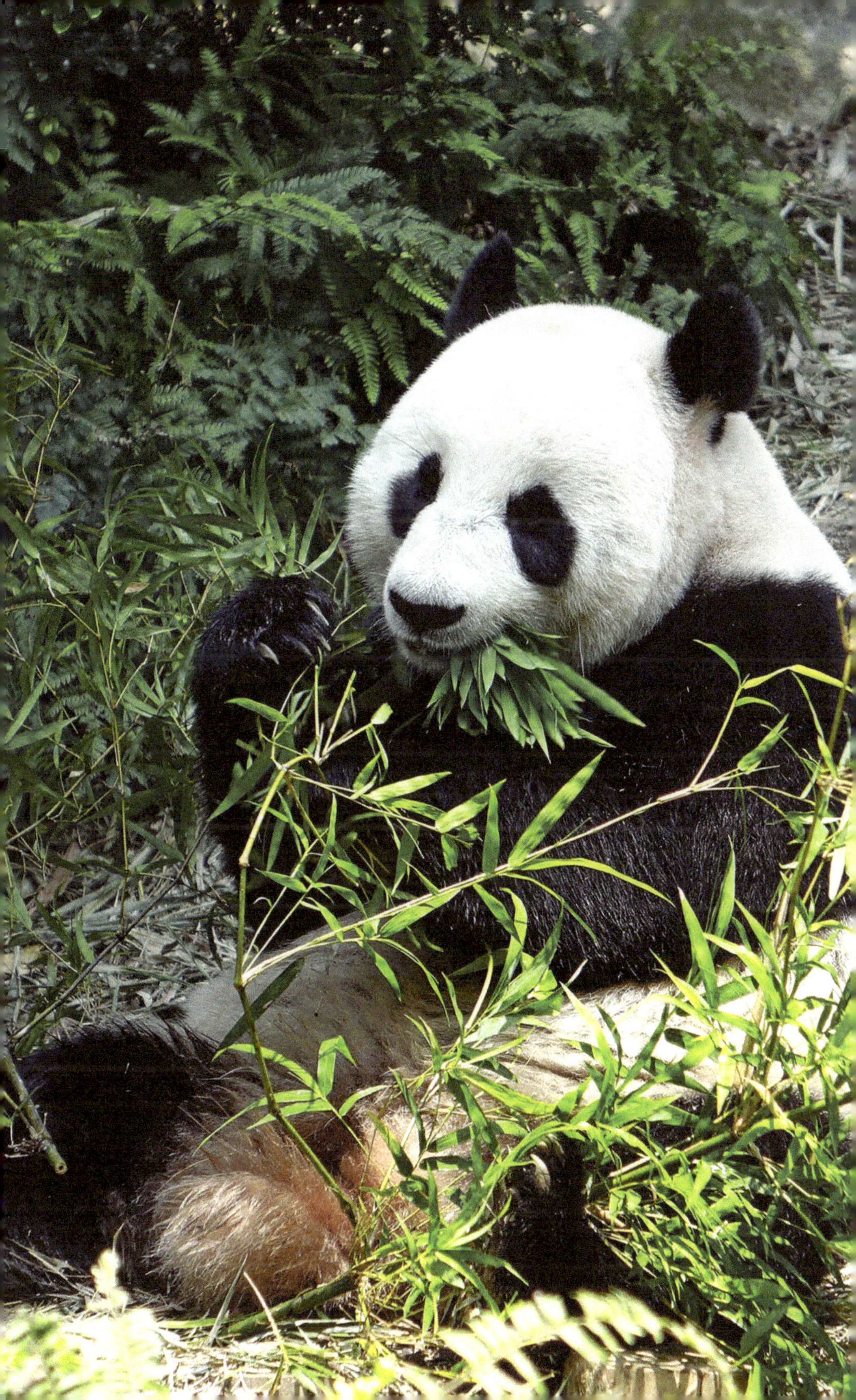

It is illegal to kill a panda. In China, the punishment is 10-20 years in prison. However, in the past, it was punishable by life imprisonment or even death.

...

Pandas can't make facial expressions. Instead, if they want to intimate another animal, they stare at them with their heads down.

...

During the first month of a cubs life, its mother never leaves it alone. She keeps it close to her and covers it with her paw or arm to protect it.

Why are pandas black and white? They are perfectly designed for camouflaging! Their mostly white bodies blend in well in snowy environments, while the black markings help them to hide in shade. The big black circles around their eyes are also believed to make their eyes look larger and more intimidating.

•••

Pandas have giant slits as pupils, which is similar to cats and different from other types of bears.

•••

Red pandas live 10-15 years in the wild.

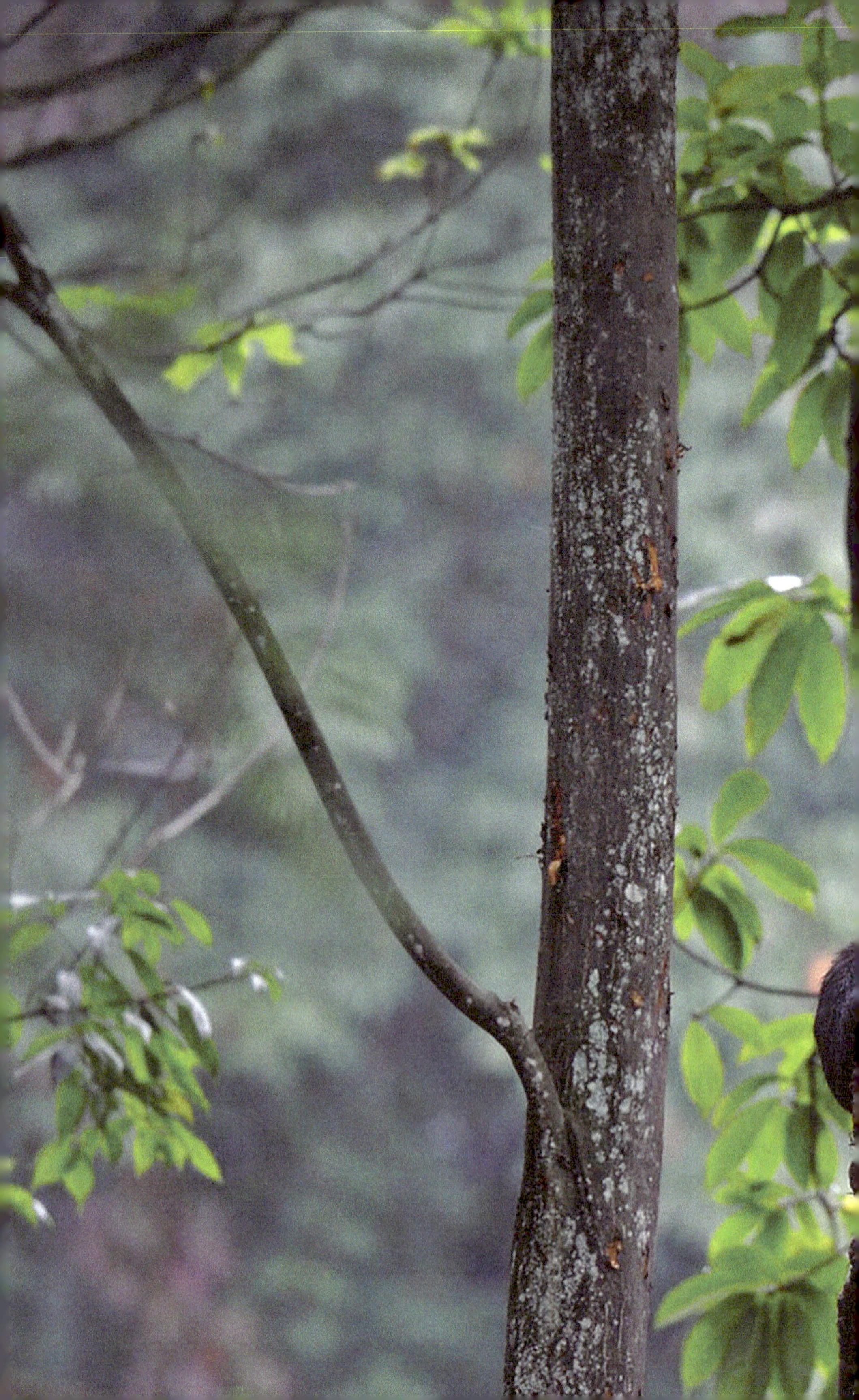

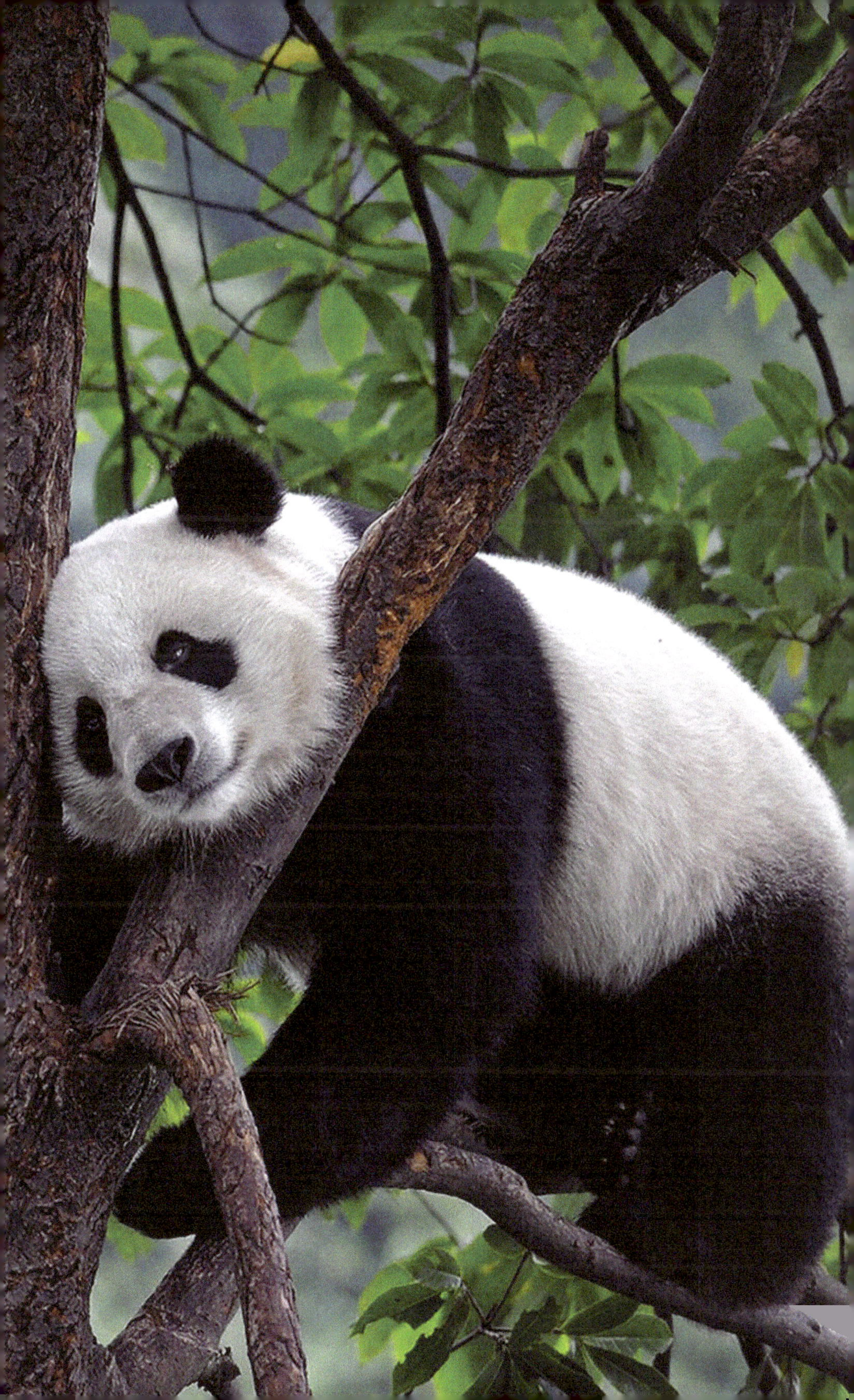

There are two subspecies of the giant panda, one of which is the Qinling panda. The Qinling panda has a light brown and white pattern and is found in the Qinling Mountains at high elevations of 1,300-3000m.

• • •

Pandas tails are the second-longest in the bear family, after the sloth. They are about 10–15 cm (4–6 in) long.

• • •

Pandas have very thick, woolly coats, which help them to stay warm during the winter months in the mountains.

A young cub practicing its climbing.

A Red Panda.

When pandas are born they have sterile intestines, meaning they can't digest their food naturally. To help them digest, they use bacteria from their mother's poop!

• • •

Most of the protein in a panda's diet comes from the leaves of bamboo. The stems have much less.

• • •

All adult pandas have their own territory, and females in particular will not let any other panda enter her territory.

Pandas are able to reproduce when they reach the age of between 4 and 8 years old. They can then continue reproducing until they are about 20 years old.

...

In August 2014, a panda gave birth to triplets in China. This is very rare, and has only been known to have happened four times.

...

In the 1970's it was common for China to gift pandas to countries such as the USA and Japanese. This was known as 'Panda diplomacy'.

Pandas may help with global warming! Scientists are researching how to use microbes in panda poop to create biofuels, which are much safer for our environment.

・・・

The Sichuan Giant Panda Sanctuaries, made of up seven nature reserves and nine scenic parks, are home to 30% of the world's panda population. It is the most important area in the world for captive panda breeding.

・・・

If you hear a mother panda tweeting like a bird, she may be anxious that her cubs are in danger.

In 2009, pandas Wang Wang and Funi arrived at the zoo in Adelaide, Australia. They are the only pandas living in the Southern Hemisphere.

•••

Like many other animals, pandas moult. While most mammals experience a 'seasonal moult', pandas don't have enough energy to do this. Instead, they undergo a continuous moult, which uses less energy. Because of this, pandas often have patchy fur.

•••

Red pandas and giant pandas have the same diet: they both love bamboo.

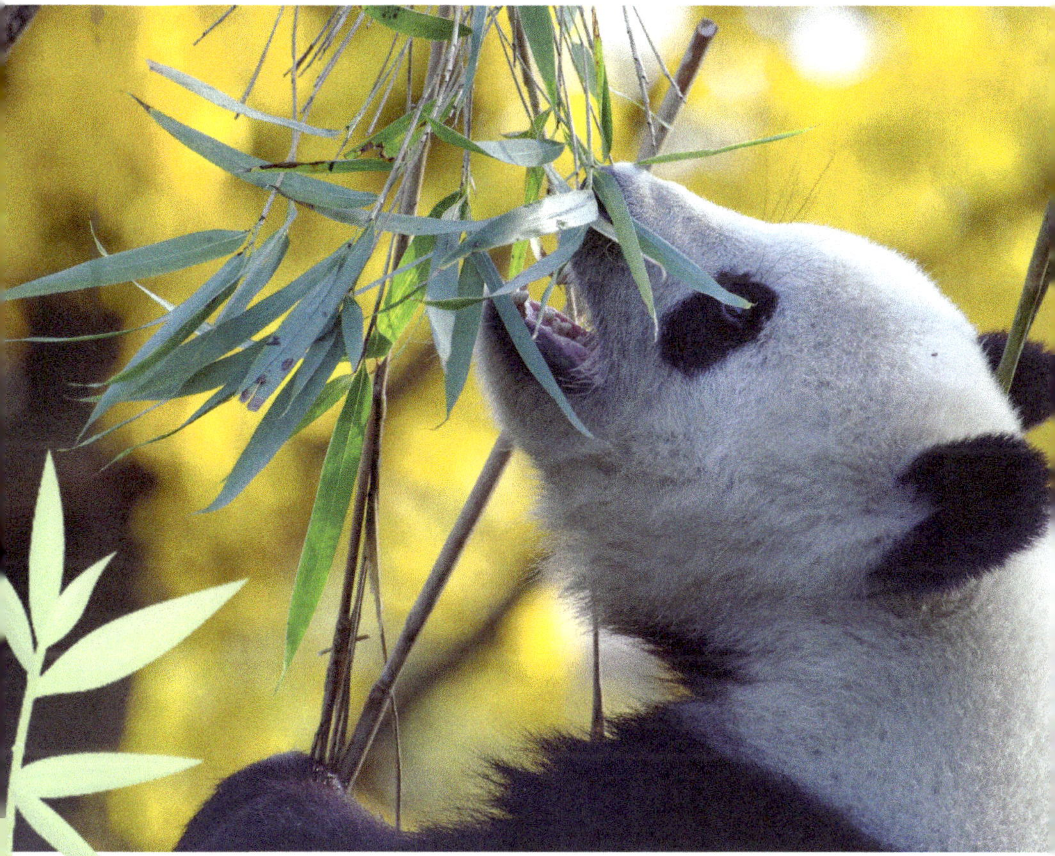

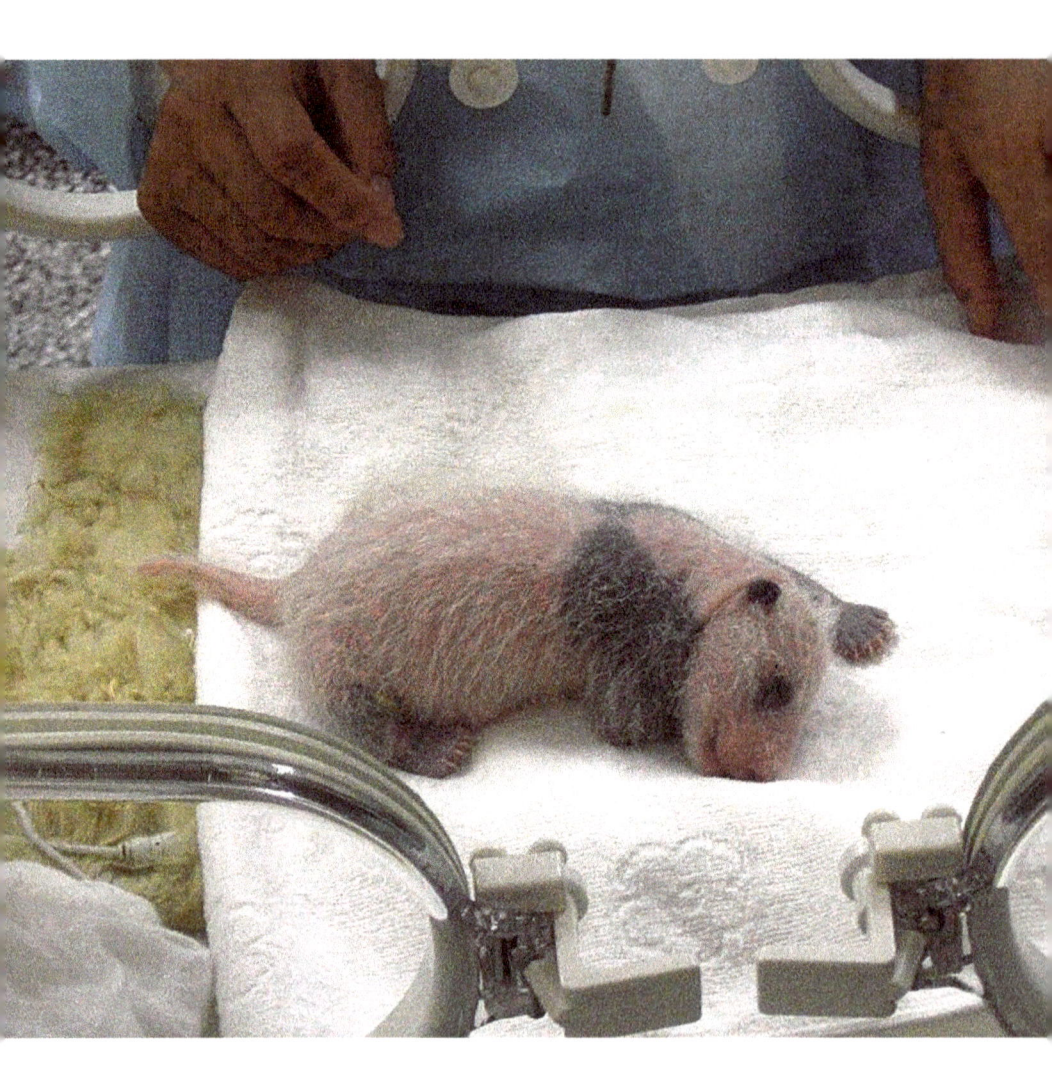

A one week old cub at Chengdu's Giant Panda Breeding Research Base.

Credit: Colegota

Why do pandas mark their territory? A pandas urine can tell another panda if they are ready to reproduce, are male or female, and how recently they were there.

...

Pandas can make some strange noises. When they are in love and trying to woo their partners, males make a 'baa' sound, like a sheep. While the female will reply with a warbling sound.

...

Pandas have featured in many television shows and movies. The animated *Kung Fu Panda* movies are particularly fun to watch!

Although adult pandas are famous for being lazy, cubs are very playful and love running and rolling around.

• • •

In 2008 a large earthquake hit the region surrounding the Sichuan Giant Panda Sanctuaries. Sadly, one panda was killed but one escaped and is still listed as missing.

• • •

Pandas are often described as 'living fossils' because they existed in almost the same form over 3 million years ago.

Red pandas can give birth to up to four cubs. They are black, blind and deaf when they are born.

• • •

Many Chinese philosophers believe that pandas are the perfect symbol of peace and harmony, due to their black and white fur that reflects Yin and Yang.

• • •

You can often see pandas rolling around. No one knows exactly why they do this. Some say that it's how they remove twigs and dirt from their fur.

Panda Quiz

Now test your knowledge in our Panda Quiz! Answers can be found on page 71.

1. What is the scientific name for the Giant Panda?

2. In which country can wild pandas be found?

3. Pandas hibernate. True or false?

4. What other colour can Giant Pandas be?

5. How many times a day do pandas poop?

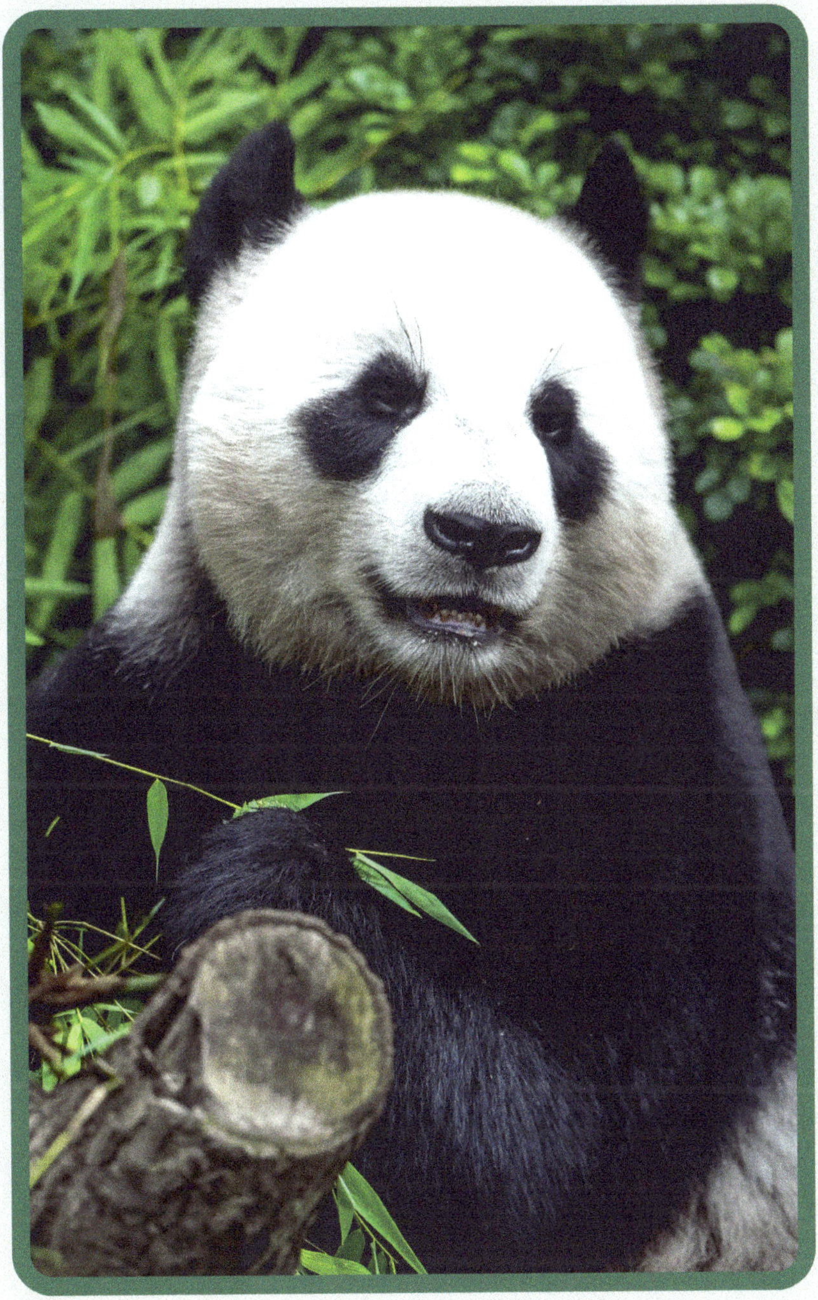

6 Do pandas prefer to live in groups or alone?

7 What family of animals does the Red Panda belong to?

8 What is the name of the panda in the WWF logo?

9 How long do panda cubs stay with their mothers before setting off on their own?

10 How many cubs do Giant Pandas usually have?

11 What colour are Giant Panda cubs when they are born?

12 At what age can panda cubs start climbing trees?

13 What do pandas have that helps them to grab bamboo better?

14 How many teeth do pandas have?

15 Pandas have quite long tails. But which bear has a longer tail?

16 Pandas also eat meat, fish and vegetables. True or false?

17 How many hours a day do pandas spend eating?

18 How many species of bamboo are there?

19 Red Pandas and Giant Pandas both love bamboo. True or false?

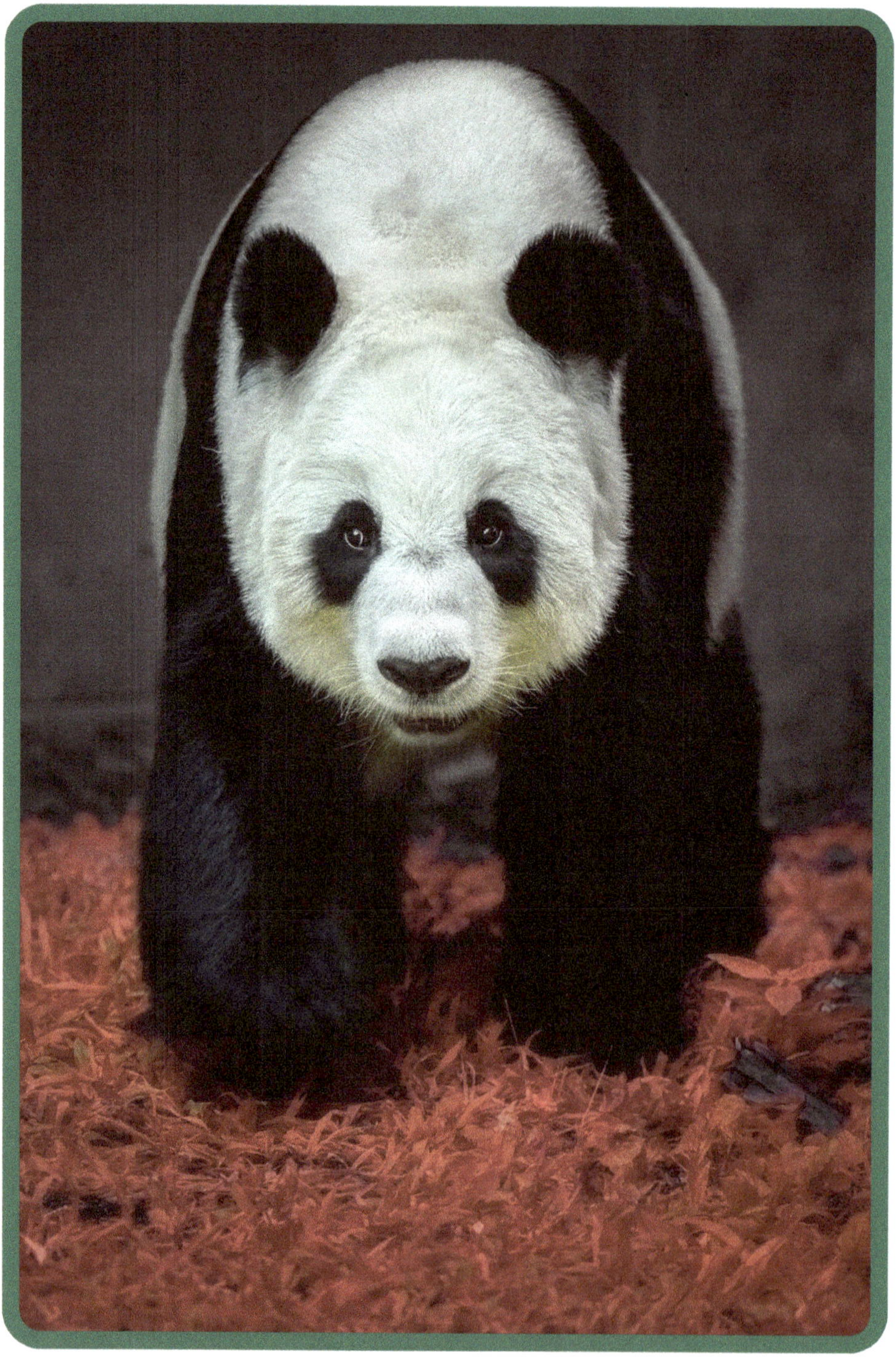

Answers

1. Ailuropoda melanoleuca.
2. China.
3. False.
4. Qinling Pandas are brown and white.
5. Around 40 times per day.
6. They prefer to live alone.
7. The raccoon family.
8. Chi Chi.
9. 18 months.
10. One. Twins are rare.
11. Pink.
12. Seven months.
13. An extra thumb, or extended wrist bone.
14. 42.
15. The sloth.
16. True
17. Up to 14 hours.
18. Over 1,000.
19. True.

PANDA
WORD SEARCH

F	D	S	Z	B	V	F	H	R	D	R	V
Y	P	A	N	D	A	E	F	A	S	E	N
T	A	Q	F	E	B	M	V	C	D	D	T
R	J	H	F	D	F	B	B	X	H	P	F
E	Q	I	N	L	I	N	G	O	B	A	S
F	Z	S	D	F	U	X	C	Q	O	N	C
C	H	E	N	D	U	F	B	V	I	D	H
V	H	B	G	Y	T	R	F	X	U	A	I
C	N	I	H	G	D	A	W	Y	Y	R	C
S	T	F	N	P	U	J	H	G	L	K	H
D	M	N	G	A	S	D	R	W	H	J	I
F	V	U	L	N	E	R	A	B	L	E	M

Can you find all the words below in the wordsearch puzzle on the left?

PANDA	QINLING	VULNERABLE
BAMBOO	CHI CHI	FLUFFY
CHINA	RED PANDA	CHENGDU

THE ULTIMATE PANDA BOOK FOR KIDS

Solution

				B				R	
	P	A	N	D	A			E	
					M			D	
			F			B		P	
	Q	I	N	L	I	N	G	O	A	
					U			O	N	C
C	H	E	N	D	U	F			D	H
	H					F			A	I
		I					Y			C
			N							H
			A							I
		V	U	L	N	E	R	A	B	L	E

Sources

"13 Interesting Facts About Giant Pandas Every Panda Lovers Want To Know". 2020. *Chinahighlights.* https://www.chinahighlights.com/giant-panda/interesting-facts.htm.

"10 Facts About Pandas! | National Geographic Kids". 2016. *National Geographic Kids.* https://www.natgeokids.com/au/discover/animals/general-animals/ten-panda-facts/.

"The Giant Panda" by *David Taylor*

"Panda Facts | Pandas International". 2020. *Pandasinternational.Org.* https://www.pandasinternational.org/education-2/panda-facts/.

Zhang, G., Swaisgood, R. R. and Zhang, H. (2004), *Evaluation of behavioral factors influencing reproductive success and failure in captive giant pandas. Zoo Biol., 23: 15–31*

Allen, Kathy. *Giant Pandas in a Shrinking Forest: A Cause and Effect Investigation. Mankato, MN: Capstone Press, 2011.*

Gannon, Megan. "Why Pandas Do Handstands When They Pee." *Business Insider*. August 28, 2012. Accessed: May 10, 2019.

Penny, Malcolm. Natural World: Giant Panda. Austin, TX: Raintree Steck-Vaugn, 2000.

"Top 10 Facts About Pandas". 2020. WWF. https://www.wwf.org.uk/learn/fascinating-facts/pandas.
Warren, Lynne (July 2006).

"Pandas, Inc". National Geographic. Retrieved 10 April 2020.

"Panda tests bring population hope". BBC. 20 June 2006. Retrieved 28 August 2020.

Dolberg, Frands (1 August 1992). "Progress in the utilization of urea-ammonia treated crop residues: biological and socio-economic aspects of animal production and application of the technology on small farms". University of Arhus. Retrieved 10 August 2020.

"Giant Panda". Encyclopædia Britannica Online. 2010. Retrieved 9 August 2020.

"Rare panda triplets born in China". cbc.ca. 12 August 2014.

"Giant Panda Vs. Red Panda". 2020. Softschools.Com. https://www.softschools.com/difference/giant_panda_vs_red_panda

@bethpylieberman, Follow. 2019. "14 Fun Facts About Giant Pandas". Smithsonian Magazine. https://www.smithsonianmag.com/smithsonian-institution/14-fun-facts-about-giant-pandas-180972879/.

We hope you learned some awesome facts about pandas!

We'd love to hear your thoughts in a review. Not only do they make us smile, but they help other readers choose the best books to buy!

Visit us at www.bellanovabooks.com for more great books, resources and regular giveaways!

THE ULTIMATE PANDA BOOK FOR KIDS

Also by Jenny Kellett

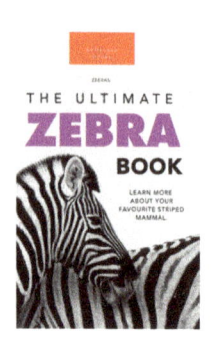

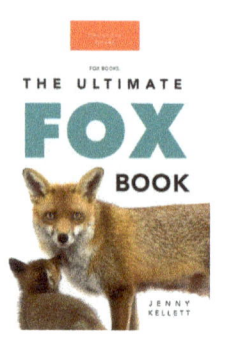

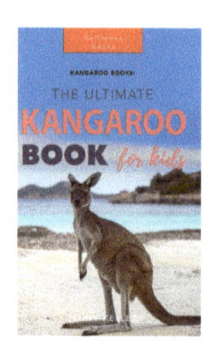

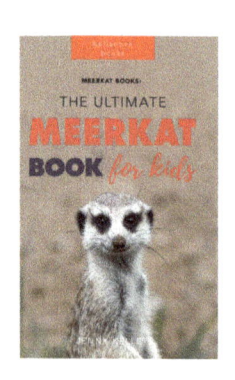

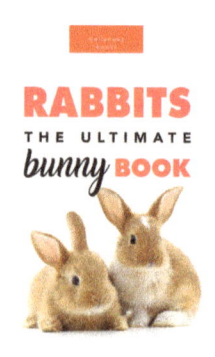

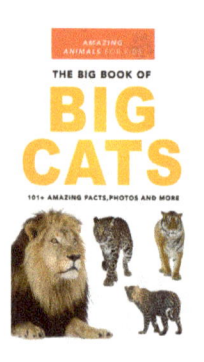

... and more!

Available in all major online bookstores